With special thanks to Martin Handford for the Where's Waldo? spread, Marissa Moss for *Heads or Tails?*, and Sam Stern for his pizza recipe

With contributions from: Andreas Samuelsson, Cristina Guitian, Matthew Hodson, Jim Medway, Nigel Coan, and Andrew Wightman

Produced by Nick Stanhope
Art direction and design by New Future Graphic
Written by Tanis Taylor and 4,386 children (more or less)

First U.S. edition 2010

First published 2008 by Walker Books Ltd, 87 Vauxhall Walk, London SE11 5HJ
and Short Books Ltd, 3A Exmouth House, Pine Street, London EC1R OJH

Library of Congress Cataloging-in-Publication Data

31 ways to change the world : we are what we do / produced by Nick Stanhope ; art direction and design by New Future Graphic ; written by Tanis Taylor and 4,386 children (more or less). —1st U.S. ed.
p. cm.
ISBN 978-0-7636-4506-9
1. Social change. 2. Change (Psychology) 3. Youth—Conduct of life. I. Taylor, Tanis. II. Title: Thirty-one ways to change the world.

HM831.T14 2010
303.48'4083—dc22   2009046533

13 14 15 16 SCP 10 9 8 7 6 5 4 3

Printed in Humen, Dongguan, China

Mixed Sources
Product group from well-managed forests and other controlled sources
www.fsc.org Cert no. SCS-COC-000927
© 1996 Forest Stewardship Council

This book was typeset in Clarendon T and Helvetica Neue.
The illustrations were done in mixed media.

Candlewick Press
99 Dover Street
Somerville, Massachusetts 02144

visit us at www.candlewick.com
www.shortbooks.co.uk
www.wearewhatwedo.org

31 Ways to Change the World

we are what we do ©

CANDLEWICK PRESS

CHANGING THE WORLD

Changing the world seems like a pretty massive task. Not the sort of thing you squeeze in before breakfast or check off while you're tying your shoelaces. "Yup, done. Next job!" Right?

Wrong! It turns out that there's tons of things you can do that don't take long at all but that can really change things.

Big things.

Like global warming, bullying, animal rights, and making people smile. **Curious?**

You do things every day. Small things that don't even take five minutes. Let's call them **actions**. You take showers. You eat chicken fingers. You buy stuff. You fart.

Over one lifetime, these actions add up. You will spend **6,000 hours in the shower.** You will eat **1,201 chickens** (or nutloaves if you're a vegetarian). You will buy **678,740 things.** (Wow!) And you will fart **421,575 times.** (Now, that's not to be sniffed at.)

You have a HUGE impact on the world around you. Every day, your actions and your choices influence other people— from your friends and your parents to chicken farmers and factory workers halfway around the world.

So in those few minutes when you're brushing your teeth or choosing an apple from the supermarket, you're having an effect that could last, well, maybe forever.

At **We Are What We Do,** we believe that by making small changes to your everyday actions, you can make a BIG difference.

When lots and lots of us make small changes to our everyday actions, then together we can

CHANGE THE WORLD.
Amazing!

In other words:

small actions x lots of people
= BIG CHANGE

Where did we get the thirty-one actions in this book? We asked the most imaginative people we knew for some ideas. We asked you. We got tons of children (well, 4,386) to give us their suggestions and handpicked the best gems. Thirty-one amazing, everyday actions. By children. For children.

Actions that everyone can do. In short amounts of time. To change the world.

They are small.
They are strange.
But do them with others,
and things will change.

Go on. Get started. Try Erica's Action #15 and teach your granny to text. Why? Because when you do it, you get to spend time with someone from a different generation. Because if we all did it, there would be millions of grandparents who could stay in touch better. Because you know stuff. And grandmas know stuff. And because we should all swap stuff. Unplug Sammah's Action #22. Pump up Omar's Action #29. Give away Emma's Action #20. And when you're done, pester everyone into doing YOUR amazing Action #31.

Find five minutes between picking your nose and cleaning out your hamster's cage and give one a try.

You can change anything and everything that matters to you—from how your house recycles and how green your teacher is to how fat your dad is and how happy your friends are.

Start here . . . continue online at www.wearewhatwedo.org and out there in the world. . . . And who knows where it will end? Happy world changing!

Make someone smile

Q: What color is a burp?
A: Burple

Continue   More

There are some people who hardly ever smile. You could call them grumps. We call them challenges.

Make someone smile — for no reason in particular.

Some say it takes half as many muscles to smile as it does to frown.

Thank you for a delicious lunch

How do you catch a squirrel?

Climb a tree and act like a nut!

You see 300 people every day. If one million kids smile at 300 people each, every person in the United States will get smiled at.

I saw this and I thought of you X

YO, WHAT'S UP?

Walk your dad

Like dogs, grown-ups get cranky when they stay inside all ⊙ DAY LONG. Unlike dogs—who walk an average of 676 miles a year—dads walk just 197. KEEP them off the furniture: take a grown-up for A WALK.

6

Illustration by Cristina Guitian

Grow something & eat it

Take a tiny seed and turn it into something amazing. Go on. I dare you.

Why not try basil? It's easy to grow and tastes great — especially on pizza!

All you need are some seeds, a sunny windowsill, and a pot of nice soil with a hole in the bottom.

Make sure you keep your seedlings watered but not too wet.

Wow! It's growing! HOORAY!

HOME-GROWN FOOD:
It's easy! It's free!
It's amazing!
No wasteful packaging!
No supermarket lines!
WARNING:
May contain bugs.

As soon as there are plenty
of leaves, pinch them off
and scatter them on top
of Action #10.

Stand up for something

If a friend was being bullied, you could wait for someone else to do something.

If your school wasn't recycling, you could wait for your principal to do something.

If the planet was heating up, you could wait for the government to do something.

Personally, we hate waiting.

Speak up.

Change your world.

Starting now.

Turn things off when you leave the room

Have you ever spotted those little red lights? Your TV, computer, and stereo seem off, but there's still a little red glow. Did you ever wonder what that was? Well, it's not a street light for a mouse. It's showing you that energy is still being used. Make sure you unplug items when you're not using them, and you will reduce electricity use in your house by up to 10 percent.

Test your teacher

FED UP WITH BEING TESTED BY YOUR TEACHERS? LET'S SEE HOW THEY LIKE IT.

SEE HOW THEY DO IN YOUR FAVORITE SUBJECT—PLANET SAVING. MOSTLY C's? NOT GOOD ENOUGH. CHALLENGE THEM TO IMPROVE, THEN TEST THEM AGAIN.

"WHAT IS IT, TEACHER? YOU NEED A BATHROOM BREAK?" SIGH. "DIDN'T YOU JUST HAVE ONE?"

At home

1. How many of your lightbulbs are low-energy?
   a. All
   b. Some
   c. None

2. What temperature setting do you normally use to wash your clothes?
   a. Cold
   b. Warm
   c. Hot

3. Are you a composter?
   a. Yes
   b. No
   c. A what?!

4. How often do you leave your appliances on standby?
   a. Never
   b. Sometimes
   c. Always

5. Do you charge your cell phone overnight?
   a. Never
   b. Sometimes
   c. Always

6. Do you turn the faucet off while you brush your teeth?
   a. Always
   b. When I remember!
   c. Never

Getting around

1. How do you get to school?
   a. Walk, bike, or public transportation
   b. In a car full of people
   c. In a car on my own

2. How often do you check that your tires are pumped up to the right pressure levels? (Helps your car use less gas!)
   a. Regularly
   b. Occasionally
   c. Never

3. How do you travel on the weekend if your trip's less than a mile?
   a. Walk or bike
   b. Public transportation
   c. Car

4. How many airplane flights do you take every year?
   a. None
   b. One or two
   c. More than three

At school

1. Do you use both sides of the paper when you photocopy?
   a. Always
   b. Sometimes
   c. Never

2. Do you have recycling bins in the staff room?
   a. Yes, for everything!
   b. Yes, for paper
   c. No, none

3. What do you pour your coffee into?
   a. A reusable mug
   b. A paper cup, once a day
   c. A paper cup, multiple times a day

4. Do you print on recycled paper?
   a. Always
   b. Sometimes
   c. Never

How did you score?

Mostly a's: Bright Green. Well done! Bravo. You are qualified to teach me in the ways of the world, as you are a big, green, shining beacon. Teacher, I salute you.

Mostly b's: Light Green. You might know your stuff in the classroom, but you won't win any prizes for planet saving. Strong start, but you must try harder.

Mostly c's: Limp Green. Oh, dear, we have a problem. If this doesn't improve, not only will the planet go "pop" but you will also have to see me after class.

Look closer

Sometimes it pays to take your time—to look
closer, to notice things no one else does.
It makes you good at Where's Waldo?
It makes you good at life.

Ten of our actions have wandered into
Waldo's world. Can you find them? (And him?)

Be friendly in sign language

"Hello!"

A bit of sign language always comes in handy. Use it in quiet places (libraries). Use it in loud places (football games). Use it to make friends with hundreds of thousands of people who use American Sign Language (ASL) in their daily lives.

"I'm glad to meet you!"

Say hello by moving your hand, palm out, from the side of your face outward.

Then tell a new friend you're happy to meet her by patting your chest twice and bringing the index fingers of your hands together.

Layer up

What is our greatest weapon against global warming?

Science? Biofuel? Solar power?

Nuh-uh. It's a sweater. The next time it gets chilly, put a sweater on.

Not the heat.

Setting the thermostat just one degree lower than usual can save 3 percent of the energy used to heat your home.

Is your central heating making you fat? When our houses are cooler, our bodies burn more calories to keep us nice and toasty.

The first radiator was invented in 1855. Before that, people wore bigger sweaters. And hugged more.

21

Cook a meal from scratch

Your mission, should you choose to accept it, is dinner for two. Cook it from scratch. Using only raw ingredients.

Your secret weapon? Sam Stern, teenage chef. Good luck.

(And call us when it's ready.)

SAM'S MARGHERITA PIZZA - SERVES 2

PIZZA CRUST:

3 ⅓ CUPS BREAD FLOUR
1 TSP SALT
1 TSP SUGAR
2 .25-OUNCE PACKAGES
 ACTIVE DRY YEAST
1 ¼ CUPS WARM WATER
2 TBSP OLIVE OIL

PIZZA TOPPING:

1 CLOVE GARLIC, CRUSHED
14 ½-OUNCE CAN
CHOPPED TOMATOES
2 BALLS FRESH
MOZZARELLA
CHEESE, SLICED

A FEW BLACK OLIVES
SALT AND BLACK PEPPER
OLIVE OIL

A FEW LEAVES OF
ACTION #3

1. PREHEAT OVEN TO 400°F. SIFT FLOUR AND SALT INTO A BOWL. ADD SUGAR AND YEAST.

2. POUR IN WATER AND OLIVE OIL. WORK DOUGH INTO A SOFT BALL. ADD A DROP MORE WATER IF NEEDED.

3. SLAP DOUGH ONTO A LIGHTLY FLOURED BOARD. PUNCH, PULL, THUMP, AND KNEAD FOR 10 MINUTES UNTIL SOFT AND ELASTIC.

4. LEAVE COVERED IN A WARM PLACE FOR 1 HOUR, OR UNTIL DOUBLED IN SIZE.

5. LIGHTLY OIL TWO BAKING TRAYS. DIVIDE DOUGH INTO TWO EQUAL BALLS AND ROLL OUT FLAT. LEAVE COVERED ON BAKING TRAYS TO RISE AGAIN FOR 15 MINUTES.

6. MIX GARLIC INTO CHOPPED TOMATO, AND SPREAD ON CRUSTS.

7. SCATTER MOZZARELLA, OLIVES, SALT, AND PEPPER. DRIZZLE WITH A LITTLE OLIVE OIL.

8. BAKE 15–20 MINUTES. SERVE WITH A SCATTERING OF ACTION #3.

Love your stuff

New stuff comes in nice packaging.

It smells good and has fancy tags.

Old stuff doesn't. It's flat from being at the bottom of your bed. Or smelly from being your favorite soccer shirt. It's full of holes—and you've earned every one of them.

Love your stuff. To bits.

I love snakey 'cause he scare my brother.

I have had her for a long time

I love taking pictures of things that I love.

I've had it since I was a baby.

This turtle reminds me of my grandda

He's got good clothes.

It reminds me of being in Portugal.

Soccer is my best subject.

I love Tom because I got him when I was a baby.

I will always love her.

He can be moody but I don't care.

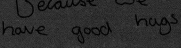

she is always happy.

Because we have good hugs.

This is my first trophy.

Go to more parties

Merry Bean-Throwing Day!

Happy Diwali!

Groundhog Greetings!

The great thing about having friends from other cultures is that you get to go to all their parties. We've taken the liberty of putting a few dates on your calendar.

JANUARY

Burns Night
A Scottish celebration of the life of poet Robert Burns on January 25th (Robert Burns wrote "Auld Lang Syne." All together now . . .)

The Lantern Festival
On the fifteenth day of the first month, the streets are lit with glowing, colorful lanterns to mark the end of the Chinese New Year and welcome new beginnings. Children stroll the streets holding homemade lanterns.

FEBRUARY

Groundhog Day
If the groundhog emerges from his burrow on February 2nd and doesn't see his shadow, it means winter will soon end. If he does see his shadow, it's back into his hole, and winter for six more weeks. Boo.

Carnival
Seven weeks before Easter every year, the streets of Rio de Janeiro in Brazil come alive with parties, festivals, and samba bands. The crowds wear colorful outfits covered with feathers and sequins, and children practice for months to perform in dancing bands.

Rissun

This Shinto celebration on February 3rd marks the end of winter and the chasing away of evil spirits. People throw handfuls of beans into any dark corners while shouting, "Fortune in, devils out!"

MARCH

Saint David's Day

Saint David is the patron saint of Wales, and March 1st is his feast day. People celebrate Welsh culture and history and wear daffodils or leeks in their lapels

Dolls' Festival

A day for girls! In Japan, young girls display dolls in traditional dress on a platform in their house. Throughout the festival, families visit shrines to pray for girls' health and happiness.

Holi

This Hindu festival from India is nicknamed the Festival of Colors because during the day people spill out onto the streets and throw huge amounts of colored powder and water at one another!

APRIL

Children's Day

This day is celebrated throughout Turkey to remind people that children are the future. Turkish children dress in national dress and perform in plays and musicals, and the government is run by children for the day.

Vaisakhi

One of the most important holidays in the Sikh calendar, this is a time to remember the birth of Sikhism in 1699. People clean and decorate their local *gudwara*s, Sikh places of worship, with flowers and bathe themselves to purify body and soul before celebrating with parades, dancing, and singing. Children start the practice of charity on this day and continue it throughout the year.

Pesach

Pesach, or Passover, is an eight-day feast celebrating the end of slavery for the Jewish people and their arrival in Israel. People eat matzoh, a flatbread, to remind them that when they left Egypt, it was in such a rush that their bread didn't have time to rise.

MAY

Cheese Rolling

Since the nineteenth century, competitors in Gloucestershire, England, have taken part in this event: a round of Double Gloucester cheese is rolled from the top of a steep hill and they all try to catch it. Since the cheese can reach speeds of 70 miles per hour, this is quite a challenge!

Baby-Jumping Festival

In the village of Castrillo de Murcia in Spain, grown men dressed as devils leap over a row of helpless babies! As they jump, they take all the evil with them and cleanse the children.

Vesak

The most important event of the Buddhist calendar, Vesak, or Buddha's Day, celebrates the Buddha's birth, death, and enlightenment. Homes are cleaned and decorated. Flowers, candles, and joss sticks are left at the feet of statues. People eat vegetarian food, and caged animals, insects, and birds are ceremonially freed.

Dragon Boat Festival

When a famous Chinese poet named Qu Yuan was drowned, the townsfolk took to their boats, beating drums and throwing dumplings into the water to scare away fish and stop creatures from eating his body. Today, teams of twenty-two paddlers take to the water in long dragon boats and race to the sound of drums.

Alien Festival

Legend has it that a UFO crashed in Roswell, New Mexico, in 1947, and each year people dressed as aliens go there to parade and party. The truth is out there . . . somewhere.

Tomato Fight

The biggest food fight in the world, this Spanish festival involves more than 200,000 pounds of tomatoes being thrown at anyone you can manage to hit. "Hey slowpoke, ketchup!"

Summer Solstice

Solstice comes from the Latin for "sun stands still," and the summer solstice is when the sun is at its highest elevation of the year. The Celts celebrated with bonfires to add to the sun's energy, and in England today, pagans and druids dance and light fires to greet the sunrise at Stonehenge's stone circle.

Grandmothers' Festival

A grand old celebration of grandmothers in Norway, this festival features grannies riding motorbikes and racehorses, skydiving, and scuba diving.

Raksha Bandhan

A Hindu festival for brothers and sisters marked by the tying of a holy thread by a sister onto her brother's wrist. In return, the brother promises to look after her, and they feed each other sweets. (No brother? No worries! Any male can be "adopted" as a brother for the occasion.)

World Pillow-Fighting Championships

Competitors sit, facing each other, on top of a slippery pole above a mud pit. Using only a pillow, they must unseat their opponent. Rounds last one minute. Feathers will fly!

Highland Games

What better way to celebrate Scotland than these games that came down from the Highlands? Cabers (long pine logs) are tossed and heavy stones thrown while bagpipes are played and kilts are worn.

Ramadan

Ramadan is a month of fasting from sunrise to sunset. During Ramadan, Muslims pray and fast, celebrating the time when the verses of the Koran were revealed to the Prophet Muhammad. The holiday of Eid ul-Fitr marks the end of Ramadan.

Ethiopian New Year's Day

The start of the New Year in Ethiopia on September 11th is a colorful affair, with priests walking around their churches with bright umbrellas and colorful holy books. Rastafarians around the world believe that Ethiopia is their spiritual homeland, so they celebrate, too.

Diwali

Diwali is the Festival of Light, celebrated by Sikhs, Hindus, and Jains. In India, the festival is a time for cleaning the home, wearing new clothes, and, most important, decorating buildings with lights.

Monkey Buffet

In Thailand, locals gather together and put out a magnificent buffet of fruit and vegetables for the monkeys that roam free. Around 600 of them turn up to take advantage of this free meal!

NOVEMBER

DECEMBER

OCTOBER

Halloween

Legend has it that, on October 31st, the boundary between the dead and the living gets blurred. So to confuse those dastardly spirits, dress as a ghoul yourself! Boo!

Oktoberfest

A jolly German festival when women wear a traditional outfit called a *dirndl* and men wear *lederhosen,* or leather shorts. Meat is eaten, beer is drunk, and there is much singing and good cheer.

Day of the Dead

Mexican people pray to the souls of dead relatives on this day and ask them to return for one night. They decorate their homes with skulls, dress as skeletons, and parade through the streets. Bread is even baked in the shape of a skull! This festival remembers dead relatives and celebrates their lives.

Christmas

An annual Christian holiday that celebrates the birth of Jesus. Children receive gifts and cards from Santa Claus, and Christmas trees are dressed with baubles and decorations and topped with a star to represent the Star of Bethlehem from the Nativity story.

Santa Lucia

On December 13th, one of winter's longest, darkest nights, girls in Sweden dress up as Santa Lucia in a white dress and a crown of candles. Boys may also dress as gingerbread men. The day is a big feast day, with lots of sweet Lucia buns eaten in celebration.

Ask "Why?"

Years ago someone looked up into the night sky and asked, "Why can't we build something powerful enough to take people to the moon?" The rest, as thay say, is history.

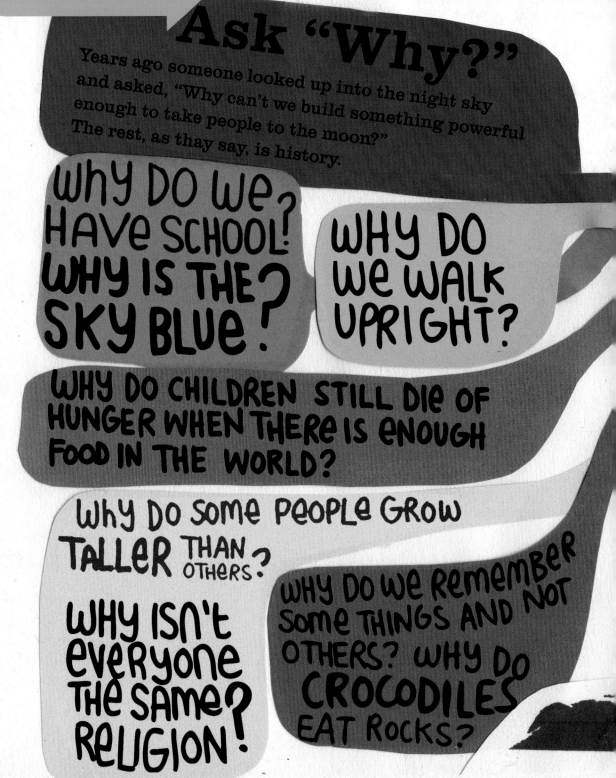

WHY DO WE HAVE SCHOOL? WHY IS THE SKY BLUE?

WHY DO WE WALK UPRIGHT?

WHY DO CHILDREN STILL DIE OF HUNGER WHEN THERE IS ENOUGH FOOD IN THE WORLD?

WHY DO SOME PEOPLE GROW TALLER THAN OTHERS?

WHY ISN'T EVERYONE THE SAME RELIGION?

WHY DO WE REMEMBER SOME THINGS AND NOT OTHERS? WHY DO CROCODILES EAT ROCKS?

Illustration by Marcus Walters

MARKS THE SPOT

Love where you live

Maps can be boring, but they don't have to be.

Why not make your own map? Fill it with places you've discovered and things you love around where you live. Fill it with stuff other kids would actually want to know.

Put your neighborhood on the map!

GOOD HILL TO RIDE DOWN REALLY FAST !!!

WOOF WOOF WOOOF GRR

WHERE U LIVE!

Illustration by Ned Selby

Teach Your Granny to Text

IMD=In my day...
NE14T?=Anyone for tea?
FDLSTX=fiddlesticks
RNGO2NITE?=Bingo tonight?

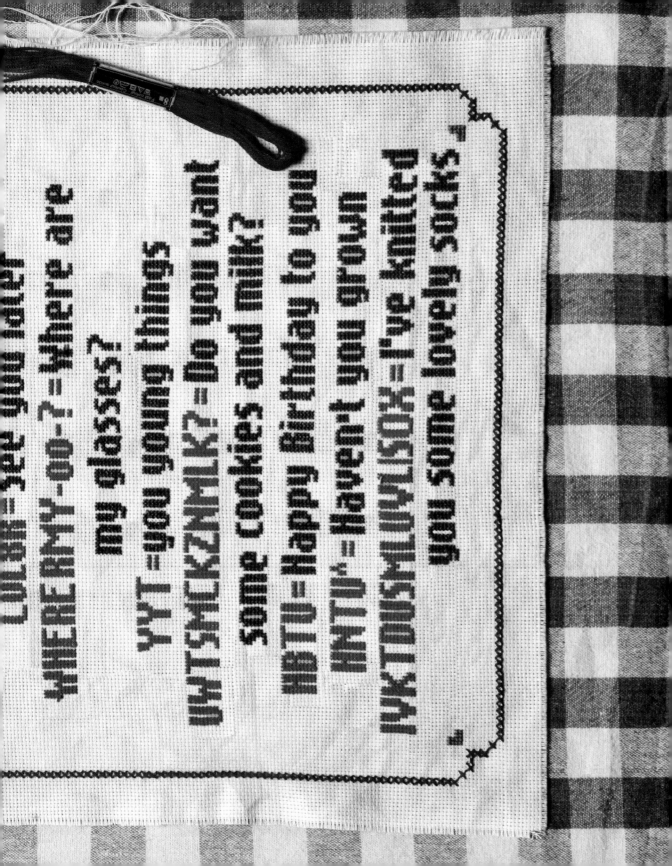

CULUR = See you later

WHERERMY-oo-? = Where are my glasses?

YYT = you young things

UWTSMCKZNMLK? = Do you want some cookies and milk?

HBTU = Happy Birthday to you

HNTU⁺ = Haven't you grown

I'VKTDUSHLUVLSOK = I've knitted you some lovely socks

Find out about your food

Our food had a whole life before it reached our table.

What's your apple's life story?

I never had what you would call my own room. I grew up on a "farm" with 30,000 other chickens. I can tell you, it's good preparation for being in a chicken sandwich, being squashed up with that crowd. I hear there are other farms where chickens get more space. To perch, peck, cluck about. I dunno. Sounds egg-straordinary to me.

I started life as a cocoa bean in Ghana. Life was sweet. And by the time I was picked and sugared, so was I. Our farm is fair-trade-certified, which means a fairer price for us beans. It also means a better future for our farmers. And more whistling. Whistling isn't an essential ingredient in chocolate. But I think it helps.

I was born and raised in an orchard just around the corner, so I feel pretty at home here. Some of my friends at the supermarket came all the way from a place called New Zealand. It took them ages to get here. My friend Adam the Apple said he hated flying all that way. I don't blame him. They had to come more than 8,000 miles, and the in-flight movies sucked. Ridiculous.

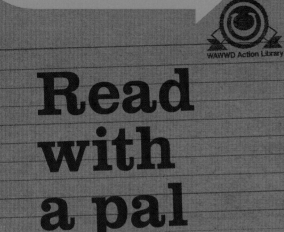

WAWWD Action Library

Read with a pal

It's just plain rude to keep a good story to yourself....

HEADS OR TAILS?
Marissa Moss

THIS WAS THE THIRD TIME in a row I'd won the coin toss. That meant I got to read the comic first again. See, Omar and I always pool our money and buy comics together, which means we get more pages per penny, but we also have to share, as in taking turns reading. You'd think we'd have a system, like first me (of course, first me), then Omar, then me again. But it's not

like that. Each time we get a new comic, we flip a coin to decide who gets it first.

My older brother, Kevin, says that's a stupid way to do things, but then he thinks practically everything I do is stupid — even reading comics, which is definitely one of the least stupid things I do. I think comics are great. You get words *and* pictures all wrapped up together, plus excitement and humor. I've read plenty of boring books (mostly for school), but I've never read a boring comic.

Omar agrees with me. That's one reason we're best friends. We like the same things. I feel kind of bad walking home from the comic store with him because I know how much he wanted to get first dibs, especially since he lost the last two times. But hey, a coin toss is a coin toss.

"I promise I'll read it fast — tonight, even," I say.

"OK," Omar says, but he seems annoyed about losing.

I try to cheer him up. "Want to work on *our* comic now?"

That's another thing Omar and I do together. We not only buy comics; we also make them. We just finished drawing "Alien Eraser and the Voice of Doom." We have a whole series with Alien Eraser, who is a handy-dandy pencil-top eraser with a lot of alien personality. He's small and turquoise with typically alien big slanty eyes and incredible powers, so many we haven't discovered all of them yet. We're pretty sure Alien Eraser built the pyramids of Egypt and those mysterious giant heads on Easter Island, and he knows how to time-travel through intergalactic wormholes, but we haven't written about that stuff yet.

You may think it would be hard to write and draw something with another person, but if the other person is your best friend, if the other person is someone like Omar, it's usually easy. We sit at the kitchen table together (at his house or mine—it doesn't matter which), and get out some paper, and one of us starts to write and draw. We both decide what's going to happen, what Alien Eraser will say, what dangers he'll face. We both draw, too, sometimes handing the pencil over after one panel, sometimes after a whole page. It doesn't really matter who does the pictures and panels, but we each have our specialties. Omar is great at spaceships, so he always draws that part, but if there's a monkey or a dog or a gorilla, then the pen is mine! I think I'm especially good at poodles. Too bad that so far there hasn't been one in our comics. Next time, I always think, but there hasn't been a place for a poodle character yet.

Like I said, usually working together is easy, but today is different. When we go to Omar's house after the comic store, we spread out our paper and pens. But that's about as far as we get. No matter what I suggest, Omar doesn't like my ideas.

"How about Alien Eraser gets all the other stuff in the confiscation drawer to mutiny against the evil teacher?" I say. "They could tie her up and stick her in the closet, like she's being confiscated herself! That would be funny!"

"That wouldn't work," says Omar. "Alien Eraser is alive, but the squirt guns and gum and rubberband balls and other junk in the drawer aren't. They're just things. You can't suddenly make them superheroes."

"Then how about Alien Eraser uses the squirt gun to shoot himself out of the drawer on a stream of water?"

Omar rolls his eyes. "Not the old squirt gun cliché!"

"OK, then, he chews the gum in the drawer, sticks it on his feet, and climbs down using his gum-feet like suction cups." Even as I say it, I wonder how I'll draw it, but still, it could work.

"Booooooring!"

I'm beginning to get mad. I keep coming up with terrific ideas, and Omar doesn't like any of them.

"I've got it! Alien Eraser whistles a high, shrill sound that only a dog can hear, and a poodle passing by — maybe it's the janitor's dog — comes into the room and nudges open the drawer, and Alien Eraser hops onto its curly back to escape. That way I can finally draw a poodle!"

Omar snorts. "C'mon! That's the most ridiculous of all."

Now I'm really fed up. "A poodle is never ridiculous! The whole point of comics is that you can make anything you want to have happen actually happen. You're not supposed to worry about reality. If we did, there'd *be* no Alien Eraser."

I start shoving my stuff into my backpack. "Forget it. It's too hard to make a comic together if you're going to be like this."

"Wait a minute — you can't leave," Omar says. "We haven't done anything, not even one panel!" He holds up his hands as if he's trying to ward off the waves of steaming anger coming from my ears. It's like we're in a comic ourselves. I can practically see the wavy lines around my head showing fury. I can see the thought bubble over Omar's head saying "Whoa! Calm down!" I imagine that Alien Eraser is standing on my shoulder, shaking his head and muttering, "Earth boys! Who can understand them? It takes so little to drive them red with rage. And they call themselves friends? What they need is Alien Eraser's Superior Mind Control."

So I take a deep breath.

"I'm listening," I say.

"How about we flip a coin? We do that to decide who gets new comics first. We can do it to decide whose idea to use."

I think for a minute. That sounds fair. Except Omar hasn't come up with any ideas — he's just rejected all of mine. I point that out to him.

"I do have an idea!" he insists. "You never gave me the chance to say it."

"Then this is your chance."

"I agree that Alien Eraser should use the stuff in the drawer to escape, but it should be something *funny*. I mean, it is a comic! There's got to be something silly in the drawer that he turns into a serious — well, not so serious — tool for escape."

It's an OK idea, but no way am I going to admit it.

"What silly/serious tool do you have in mind?" I ask.

"How about one of those paddles with a rubber ball tied to it with string? Alien Eraser could cling to the ball and bounce himself off the paddle and out of the drawer. It would look hilarious!"

"But then he'd land with a crash," I said, "which isn't so funny." I think for a second. "What if he uses a whoopee cushion instead and parachutes down to a slightly bumpy, but not too painful landing? Maybe he could land on a poodle napping nearby."

"I like it," Omar says. "Except the poodle part. That comes out of nowhere."

"So should we flip the coin to see which ending we use?" I take a quarter out of my pocket and get ready to toss it.

"We don't need to this time. We'll use your ending. I mean, really it's *our* ending anyway. I started it—you just made it better."

I smile. "Is that an apology for being a jerk?"

"I guess," says Omar. "If you apologize for always winning when we flip a coin."

"So that's what this is about?" I ask. "It's about you losing the other coin toss, not about whether my ideas are dumb?"

"Oh, your ideas are dumb, all right." Omar grins. "Sometimes."

I'm still a little angry, but I want to finish the comic. And we're friends again, even if I'm still sore. I do like Omar's idea being combined with mine. That seems the most fair.

I'm sorry I don't get to draw the poodle, but I have fun making the whoopee cushion parachute. By the time we finish the comic, I'm not mad at all anymore.

I don't mean to do it, but my hands reach into my backpack. I take out the comic we bought after school. "Here," I say to Omar. "You read it first. I can wait."

Omar stares at me. "Really? How come?"

I shrug. "That's what friends are for."

Omar smiles. "I'll remind you of that the next time you win the coin toss." Before I can change my mind, he grabs the comic.

"Don't push your luck," I say. "Next time, I know just what's going to happen to Alien Eraser, and you'll think my idea is brilliant—I promise."

"So what's your idea?" Omar asks.

"I'm not telling you yet," I say as I head for the door. As I walk home I tell myself the story we'll put into the next issue of Alien Eraser. It's all about Mind Control and how Alien Eraser uses it to get some random Earth boy to tell his story, how he left the Planet of the Pencil Shavings and searched the universe for his next adventure, and found it right here, in our country, in our city, on our block. And somewhere on the way, he meets a poodle. It's my best idea yet, so I know Omar will love it. Or if he doesn't, there's always the coin toss.

Don't sing in the shower

The average shower lasts seven minutes and uses more than 10 gallons of water.

Actually, two minutes is all it takes to soap up, wash down, scrub your armpits, do your private parts, and still have time for your hair. If everyone in your class took two-minute showers for a year, you could fill an entire swimming pool with the water saved. And then some.

Take shorter showers. Save your singing for the rain.

(P.S. Shorter showers also mean more time to sleep in. Which is almost as good as saving the world.)

Play

OK, so we lied.
Not all the actions are in
the book. This one's outside,
waiting to happen.

You still here? Go play!

Photography: New Future Graphic

Give lots of compliments

Compliments get easier when you do them regularly, so make a five-a-day habit of giving them away. They cost nothing. They make you feel good. Everyone accepts them. And a good one can last for weeks.

1

○ VOUCHER — *Give one, get one free!*

TO: Samantha — Monday

COMPLIMENT:

I like your hair

SIGNED Selan

2

○ VOUCHER — *Give one, get one free!*

TO: Noah — march 21

COMPLIMENT: you are good in goal

SIGNED Sam

3

○ VOUCHER — *Give one, get one free!*

TO: cara thornton — monday

COMPLIMENT: I Like sitting Next to you

SIGNED Sophie B.

4

○ VOUCHER — *Give one, get one free!*

TO: Mohammed — June 1

COMPLIMENT:

You look happy

SIGNED Tahir

5

○ VOUCHER — *Give one, get one free!*

TO: Cara — 3/21

COMPLIMENT: you make me laugh

SIGNED Eugenie

Stop junk mail

HELLO.
A PIZZA FLYER? FOR ME?
YOU SHOULDN'T HAVE. . . .
NO. I MEAN IT. YOU REALLY
SHOULDN'T HAVE. YOU SEE.
EVERY YEAR 100 MILLION TREES
ARE CUT DOWN TO MAKE THE
JUNK MAIL WE GET IN THE U.S.

I DON'T MIND PIZZA FLYERS.
BUT THEY MAKE LOUSY FORESTS.

THANKS!

SLAM-DUNK THE JUNK: NO JUNK MAIL

My mailbox is on a diet - NO JUNK MAIL, PLEASE

I ♥ TREES

no junk mail, please

I'M JUNK-FREE!

Cut your junk mail by contacting companies that send unwanted catalogs, solicitations, or flyers and asking them to take you off their mailing list.

And why not make a sticker to put on your front door to tell the world — and the post office — that you're cutting out the junk?

JUNK

49

Don't charge your phone overnight

Help us.
We need
our sleep
too.

Sorry. Extra energy doesn't equal extra whizzy super powers (nice as that would be).

Most cell phones are fully charged in under two hours. But we waste millions of dollars a year charging them all night.

Don't. We all need our zzz's. That includes you, cell phone.

Illustration by Nigel Coan

51

Don't start a war

We make about 216 choices every day. Try to make the right ones.

Don't ~~worry~~ if you make a mistake

(Sometimes these things have a way of working out. . . .)

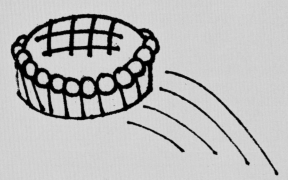

It was 1886, and pharmacist John Pemberton just couldn't get his magical medicine to work. It was supposed to cure tiredness and sore teeth, but about the only thing going for it was that it tasted good. **It was Coca-Cola.**

After little Frank Epperson stirred himself up a fruit drink in 1905, he got distracted and went off to play. The drink stood overnight on the porch.

By morning, it had frozen stiff with the spoon stuck in it. Frank thought it tasted good. **And the world had the Popsicle.**

Some college students in New England so loved the pies from the Frisbie Baking Company that they would not only eat them; they'd also play with the empty tins afterward. Their favorite game was throwing the tins to each other, yelling "Frisbie" to warn others. **It caught on.**

In 1928, Scottish scientist Alexander Fleming left an experiment by an open window. By morning, his bacteria samples had gone moldy. Instead of throwing them out, he looked closer and found that the mold was gradually dissolving the harmful bacteria. **Turns out he'd discovered penicillin—the wonder antibiotic used to save billions of lives.**

In New York in 1853, there was a very picky customer. And a very grumpy chef. The customer demanded that his potatoes be cut thinner and fried longer. Furious, the chef cut them very thin, fried them for ages, and covered them in salt. The customer asked for more. **Hooray! The potato chip was born.**

Christopher Columbus was an explorer looking for a western route to Asia. But on his way west in 1492, he bumped into an entirely different continent. He was wrong about how to get to Asia. **But he got the credit for Europe's discovery of America.**

Walking across deserts is thirsty work. So hundreds of years ago, an Arabian merchant had an idea: he'd carry his precious milk in a pouch made from a sheep's stomach. But chemicals from the pouch and the heat of the desert turned the milk into cheese. Useless if you want a drink. **But delicious on toast.**

Walking on a ship deck in 1943, an engineer watched, interested, as a coiled spring fell to the floor and sort of slinked around. Hmm, he thought. **Later he and his wife made their own spiral at home, dropped it from the top step, and watched it slinky-dink down to the bottom step. Of almost every house in America.**

Talk trash to your parents

Next time your parents say, "Haven't you cleaned your room?" say, "I'm glad you brought that up. I've been meaning to talk to you about cleaning up your habits!"

Illustration by Matthew Hodson

Glass bottles are totally recyclable. But in landfills, they will never decompose.

TIP:
You can find out more at www.earth911.com.

54%
of the waste we create winds up in landfills.

Write a letter

Why a good old-fashioned snail-mail letter?
You can't put a text message on the wall.
You can't reread a phone conversation.
And whoever heard of a love e-mail?

P.S.
Of course you *could* text, call, or e-mail.
But everyone loves a letter.

Dear Friend / Enemy / Politician / **Mom,**

I thought that I should write to you to say that: you owe me money / I'd like to be friends / I will not stand for global warming / **I owe you money**.

The situation is less than ideal, and from now on I will be: chasing you / not chasing you / writing to you every day / **begging your forgiveness**.

I hope you understand that I am: broke / ready to make a new start / a future taxpayer/ **your only child**.

Lots of love,

Me

Recycle your toys

There are millions of forgotten
toys in bedrooms all over the world.
Unused. Unloved. Under the bed.
It doesn't have to be this way. Give
them away. Swap them.

Love your toys. And when you're
done lovin' them, set them free.

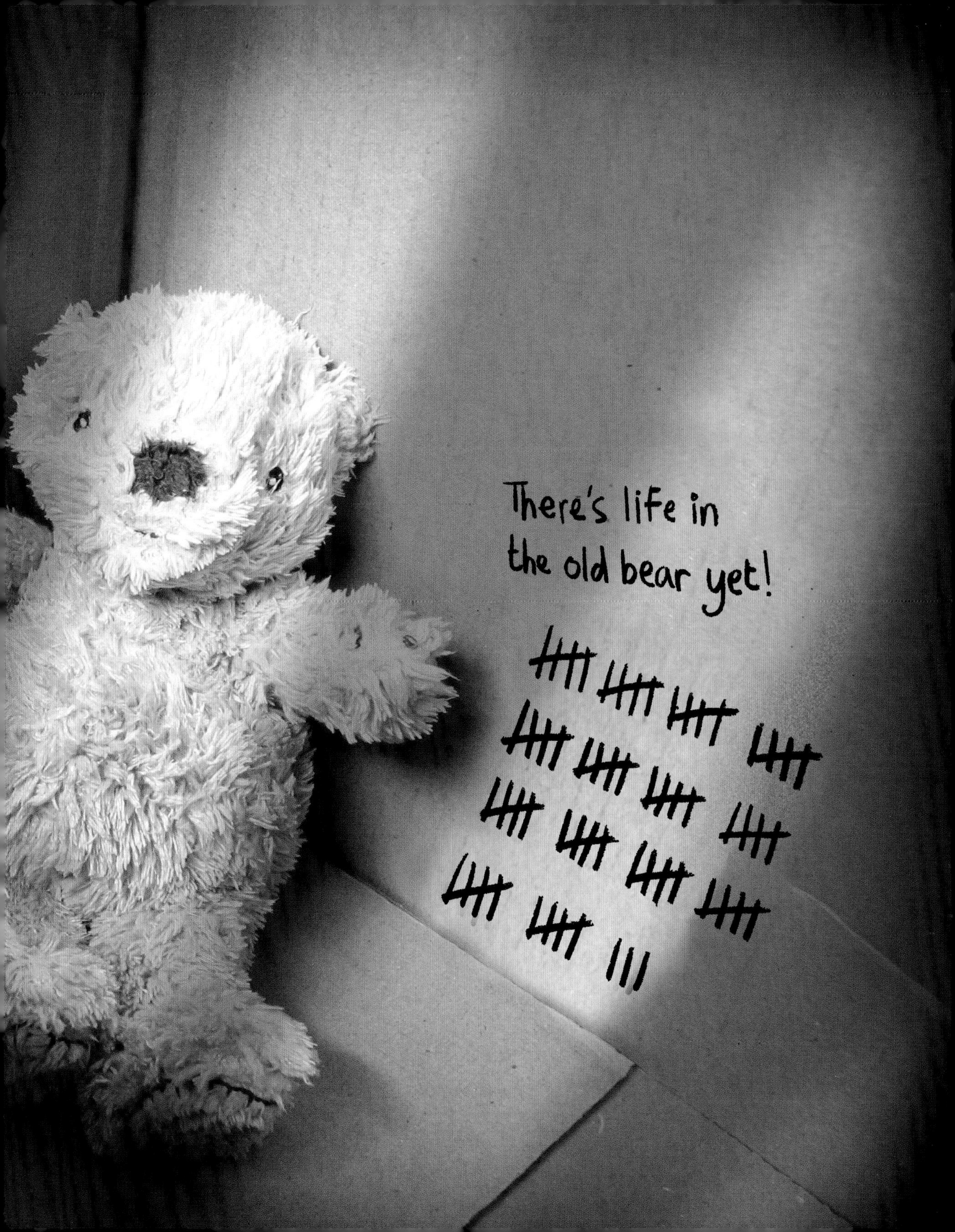
There's life in the old bear yet!

Involve everyone

Some things work better when you do them with lots and lots of people — the Wave, football games, changing the world.

This action is one of those things.

Create a story full of interesting twists and turns by adding just three words and then passing it on to someone else.
The more people you get involved, the better the story gets.

Here's one to get you in the mood.

(The only tricky part is making sure your story ends at the same place as the page!)

ONCE THERE WAS...

a bunch of apes sitting on a bus in Lincoln's Inn fields. They were visiting a little fairy called Jimmy Biggleswick. Suddenly the bus sprouted pink wings, coughed a cloud of green smoke and one ape said to another, "Why don't we get in that hot air balloon?"

As they floated an enormous winged **tape dispenser appeared.**

"Oh No! Jimmy is Stuck to the double-sided tape. Lets rescue him".

Annabel the Ape has an irrational **phobia of giant** adhesives which fly.

So she decided to blindfold herself take a knittingneedle and pop their blue spotty balloon **and red trombone**, trying to escape.

Down they fell. *The apes screamed* "What are you DOING? Silly old Annabel! And stupid phobia!! **where's my broccoli?"**

Jimmy jumps off. The tape unravels. He manages to **grab a cloud** and swing onto **the falling balloon.**

"where's my glasses?" Shouted Angus Ape **"They have disappeared!"**

"He only thinks **about his hair.** That pesky ape!"

Meanwhile, Mrs. Biggleswick catches the balloon, **uses the tape,** Says *Abracadabra* **and patches it up.** All the apes and the Biggleswicks start to breakdance. Annabel and Angus **fall in love** and all lived **happily ever after.** Broccoli and all!

Speak soccer

Yes, you're right. Soccer is a game and not a language. Silly us.

But kicking a ball around is a great way of talking to people who might not understand you.

There are 6,000 languages in the world. Soccer speaks every one of them.

CIAO

SA

ADAAB

HELLO

HOLA

WUNMAN NJINDE

Illustration by Marcus Walters

in and around

Knit
with
someone

Two needles are needed to knit,
a ball of yarn, and that's it.
As a bonus, it's true,
when knitters are two,
there's chatter and tales as you sit.

Illustration by Tori Flower

66

and through and OFF...

Add your own action

Oh, thank goodness you're here! We've been waiting for you. Holding your page. You see, we're one author short of a book. One action short, too. And it's the most important, because it's yours.

So. What's the one thing you would ask one million people to do to change the world? Take your time (writers always do). Then go tell all your friends you've just finished writing your first book.

I'd like one million people to . . .

....

....

....

....

....

....

....

Added your action?
Don't keep it to yourself.
Log on to www.wearewhatwedo.org
and tell the world.

Action #1
Make someone smile

Action #2
Walk your dad

Action #3
Grow something & eat it

Action #4
Stand up for something

Action #9
Layer up

Action #10
Cook a meal from scratch

Action #11
Love your stuff

Action #12
Go to more parties

Action #17
Read with a pal

Action #18
Don't sing in the shower

Action #19
Play

Action #20
Give lots of compliments

Action #25
Talk trash to your parents

Action #26
Write a letter

Action #27
Recycle your toys

Action #28
Involve everyone

Action #5
Turn things off when you leave the room

Action #6
Test your teacher

Action #7
Look closer

Action #8
Be friendly in sign language

Action #13
Ask "Why?"

Action #14
Love where you live

Action #15
Teach your granny to text

Action #16
Find out about your food

Action #21
Stop junk mail

Action #22
Don't charge your phone overnight

Action #23
Don't start a war

Action #24
Don't worry if you make a mistake

Don't worry

Action #29
Speak soccer

Action #30
Knit with someone

Action #31
Add your own action

I'd like one million people to . . .

Let us know how many of these you've done at

www.wearewhatwedo.org

About We Are What We Do

We Are What You Do believes that it is not just politicians, institutions and big business that change the world – it is also ordinary people like you and me.

We are creating a global movement of doing and changing; doing small actions and changing big problems.

Back in 2003, we asked a simple question: "What would you ask one million people to do to change the world?" Thousands of people responded and the result was our bestselling book, *Change the World for a Fiver – 50 actions to change the world and make you feel good*, now sold all over the world.

You might have also seen the "I'm NOT a plastic bag" shopping bags we created with Anya Hindmarch to bring to life the first action in the book, "decline plastic bags".

Find out more about all our other projects at
www.wearewhatwedo.org

Who are we?
We are what we do.

THANK-YOUS

Lots of people helped us with this book, and to each and every one of you—THANK YOU! In particular, we would like to give a huge thank-you to:

Britain's Department for Children, Schools and Families (DCSF) for their support on our original edition, *Teach Your Granny to Text & Other Ways to Change the World.*

The Times of **London** for their ideas, energy, and enthusiasm.

Special thanks to the thousands of teachers, schools, youth workers, and young people who worked with us on this book. Over 1,000 schools were involved in creating this book, and the final thirty actions were thought up by children and young people at:

Gilwern Primary School, Gwent; Whitehead Primary School, County Antrim; Ellacombe School, Devon; Dereham Neatherd High School, Norfolk; All Hallows RC Business and Enterprise College, Lancashire; Godwin Junior School, London; St. Andrew's CE Primary School, East Sussex; Ringwood School, Hampshire; St. Matthew's Academy, London; City and Islington Sixth Form College, London; St. Theresa's Catholic Primary School, Sheffield; Westgate School, Lancashire; Calverton Primary School; Community Links Southern Road After School Club, London; St. Andrew's CE Primary School; St. Mary's First School, West Sussex; The Billericay School, Essex; St. Thomas's Clapham, London; St. Mary's First School, West Sussex; St. Angela's Ursuline School, London; Merchant Taylors Junior School, Stanfield; New Vic Newham Sixth Form College, London Roxeth First and Middle School, Middlesex;

Essex Road Primary School, London; St. John the Baptist School, London; St. Mark's Catholic Primary School, Suffolk; St. Winefride's Primary School, London; Ashlawn Sixth Form, Rugby; Gateway Primary School, London; St. Theresa's Catholic Primary School, South Yorkshire; St. Joseph's RC Primary School, South Yorkshire; St. Bonaventure's, London; Hessle High School, East Yorkshire; Cwmtawe Comprehensive, Pontardawe; Tottenhall Infant School, London; Christchurch Primary School, Essex; Tollgate Primary School, London and Sudell Primary School, Darwen.

We also had some very special help from . . .

Helen Matthews, Lois Stokes, John Smith, the D'Rozzaro-Grays, Scilla Morgan, Jenny Beeching, Jenny Wilks, Fidelma Boyd , Paul Jackson, Dave Smithers, Tom Canning, Zuhayb Ahmed, Steve Wilks, Peg Probert, Ishlal Lawrence, Jane Ray, and Kate Phillips.

We are also very grateful to the Aldridge Foundation and *v,* which have supported We Are What We Do's education and youth programs.

The We Are What We Do team: Eugenie Harvey, Nick Stanhope, David Robinson, Nicole van den Eijnde, Tori Flower, Mike Daley, Ella Wiggans, and Frances Clarke

The We Are What We Do board of directors: Giles Gibbons, David Robinson, Stanley Harris, Eugenie Harvey, and Nick Stanhope

WHAT NEXT?

If you're here, it's because you either
a) got lost
b) got bored
c) are Japanese and start books from the back
or
d) have come to the end.

Of course, it's not really the end.

It's just the beginning.

This is the part where you visit us online at

www.wearewhatwedo.org

There, you can . . .

◎   Meet We Are What We Do and say "Hello!"

◎   **Put together your very own action tracker**

◎   Share all your world-changing activities with the world

◎   **Launch your own We Are What We Do creative campaign**

◎   Get hold of amazing stuff to do in class and give to your teacher (assuming that they have passed Action #6 to your satisfaction!)

◎   **Tell your Action #28 to the world**

◎   Send us your ideas for Action #31

◎   **Put your Action #14 on the map**

◎   Find out where we got all our facts, figures, and stats from